SALT
PEPPER
SEASON
SPICE

ALL THE FLAVORS OF THE WORLD

JACQUES PASQUET

ILLUSTRATED BY CLAIRE ANGHINOLFI

TRANSLATED BY ANN MARIE BOULANGER

ORCA BOOK PUBLISHERS

CONTENTS

Sweet or Spicy? 1
Salt 2
Pepper 8
Chili Pepper 14
Mustard 16
Ginger 20
Sugar 22
Cinnamon 26
Vanilla 28
Chocolate 30
Coffee 34
Tea 38
Glossary 42
Index 44

SWEET OR SPICY?

Can you think of a way to travel halfway around the world without ever leaving home? If you said television, you're right! What about the internet? For sure! But did you know there's an even easier way? The food on your plate! Or, more specifically, what goes *on* the food itself—the herbs, spices and condiments. Grocery-store aisles and pantry shelves overflow with them. And their fragrances and exotic flavors are part of our everyday life—in our food and also in our skincare products and our environment.

We've come a long way from the time when spices were used to disguise unpleasant smells. In the kitchen, they play an important role in altering and enhancing the natural flavors and aromas of food. They appeal to our senses of smell, taste and sight. And they're a must when it comes to creating an enjoyable eating experience.

Whenever our taste buds are tickled by a particular taste or smell, we're actually savoring a little corner of the world and its history.

SALT
ITS HISTORY

People in China have known how to extract salt for almost 5,000 years. For millennia, salt was a rare and precious commodity. Salt plays a leading role in many fairy tales. In some stories, it's even given magical powers. In the past, salt was rubbed on babies' lips to ward off evil spirits.

Roman soldiers were paid in salt. Hundreds of years ago in France, salt was so valuable that citizens had to pay a special sales tax on it, called the gabelle. These days salt is not only dirt cheap but also a staple in our homes.

In many places around the world, including Russia, visitors are traditionally greeted with bread and salt as a gesture of hospitality.

WHAT DOES IT LOOK LIKE?

Salt comes in many different forms. Here are a few examples.

Natural salt retains the flavor and color of the place where it was harvested. This very delicate salt is called **fleur de sel** and is named for where it comes from in France—for example, Guérande, Île de Ré or Camargue.

Refined salt typically comes from blocks of rock salt that have been purified. This gives refined salt its pure white color.

Flavored salt is mixed with other ingredients like aromatic herbs, **chili** pepper, lemon, seaweed and vanilla.

Coarse salt is extracted directly from marshes and sold in its natural form, as large, grayish-colored crystals.

A FEW RARE SALTS:

Murray River salt is harvested from Australia's longest river. Considered the finest salt in the world, it's also called **satin de sel**, or satin salt, for its softness.

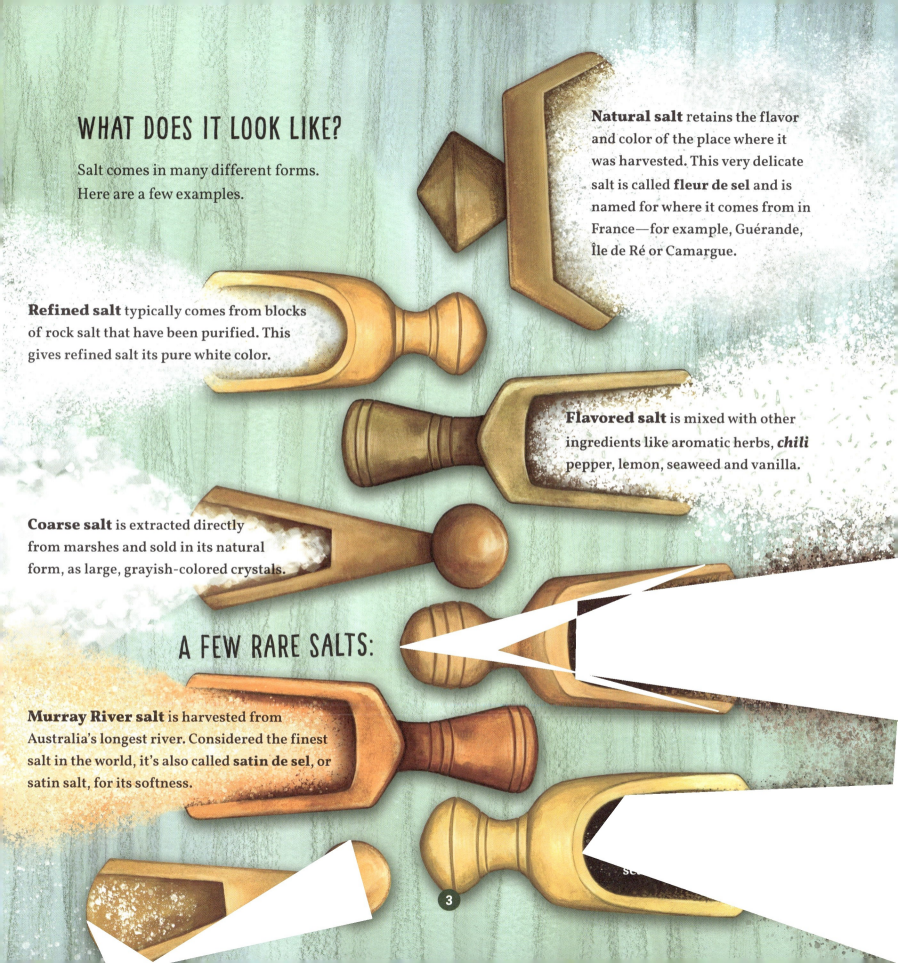

WHERE DOES IT COME FROM?

Salt comes from two main places: the ocean (sea salt) and mines (rock salt). It can also be harvested from saltwater springs.

SEA SALT

In **salt marshes**, found next to the sea, workers dig a series of interconnected ponds. The **tides** cause the seawater to flood into the marsh and travel from pond to pond. Along the way, the water evaporates under the effects of the wind and sun.

At the end of this process, workers harvest two different types of salt. On the surface of the water, at the edge of the ponds, the delicate fleur de sel is collected by hand. This fine white salt is highly prized in the field of **gastronomy**.

The remaining salt settles on the bottom of the pond in a thick, crystallized layer that's slightly gray in color. This coarse gray sea salt can be sold as is or refined to produce fine white salt.

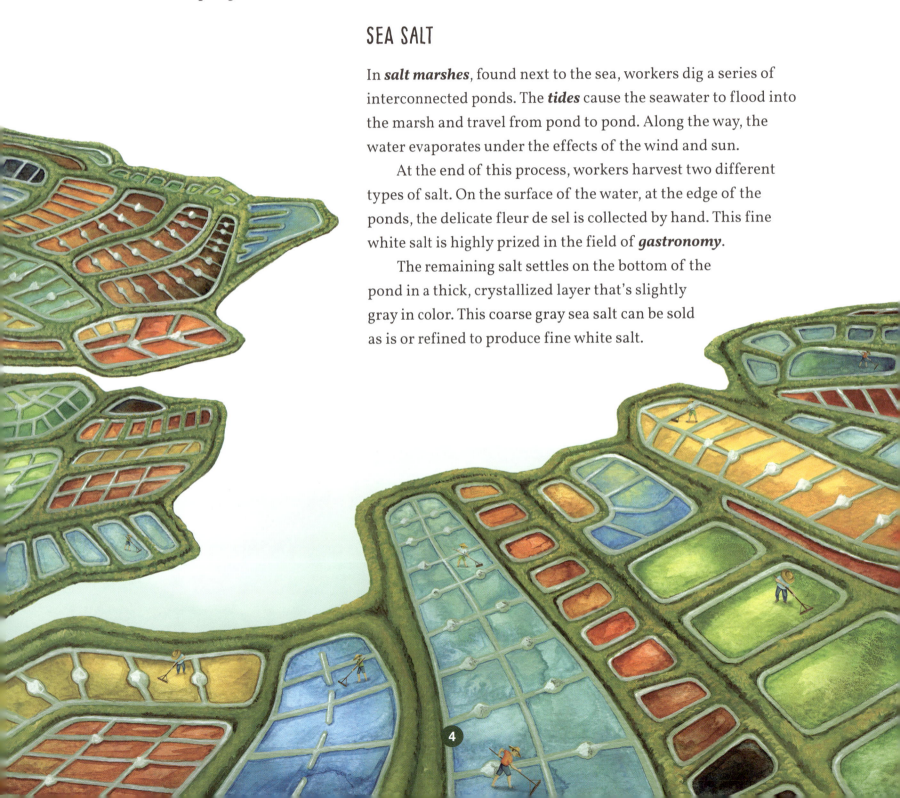

ROCK SALT

Rock salt is found deep underground in the form of solid blocks. It's extracted from quarries or mines, often in oddly shaped chunks. One example is Himalayan pink salt, a raw salt considered one of the purest in the world and highly prized by chefs. Its crystallized form has earned it the name diamond salt.

Rock salt is also used to make lamps, vases and statues.

Jordan's Dead Sea is so salty that you can practically float sitting upright in the water. The Dead Sea isn't the best place for diving, and you shouldn't even stay in the water for too long.

Contrary to its name, the Dead Sea is actually a huge saltwater lake.

Don Juan Pond in Antarctica is one of the saltiest bodies of water on Earth. It never freezes, despite its location. Salar de Uyuni, a dried-up lake in Bolivia, is the world's largest salt flat.

WHAT IS SALT USED FOR?

The first thing that comes to mind is in cooking. But why is that? It's because for centuries salt was the main way to preserve food.

Before the invention of refrigerators, **salting** meat and cheese kept them from spoiling, even on long journeys.

That's why salt is still found today in almost all food products, especially in cold cuts and prepackaged meals.

WARNING!

Too much salt is bad for your health and increases your risk of certain diseases. Processed foods and prepackaged meals are full of salt—way too much, according to doctors.

IT'S NOT JUST FOR COOKING!

Humans and animals need salt to survive. It's an essential mineral that keeps our cells, muscles and digestive systems working properly. It also helps us retain water, preventing dehydration. The salt in our bodies protects us from sunburn and heatstroke. Salt solutions can also be used to treat burn victims.

Salt is found in many common household products:
- cleaners (baking soda, bleach, water softeners)
- medical and personal hygiene products

Salt also has many industrial uses:
- road deicing
- production of textile fibers, paper pulp and glass
- production of chemicals and fertilizers

For road deicing, unrefined raw salt is mixed with sifted sand and crushed stone. But deicing causes soil erosion and increases the salt content of the groundwater, both of which are bad for the environment. New deicing techniques that are better for the environment are being developed, including one that uses sugar beet juice or a corn extract mixed with salt, and another that uses volcanic rock mixed with salt.

PEPPER

People in India and China have been using spices such as pepper, cinnamon and ginger for thousands of years. The rest of the world was limited to salt and a handful of aromatics. Black pepper first showed up in Europe in the 15th century. It became one of the most coveted spices in the world, earning it the nickname Black Gold.

Pepper was used as a form of currency to pay taxes or ransoms. Wealth was measured by how much pepper a person or a family had.

THE SPICE ROUTES

The Spice Routes is the name given to a network of trade routes used for centuries to transport all kinds of spices from Asia and the Middle East to Europe. They were made up of:
- land routes used by caravans
- sea routes discovered by sailors and used by merchant ships

Pepper and other rare spices were highly prized by many countries at the time. Wars were even fought over them. The "spice race" led to several maritime inventions, including the **astrolabe** (a navigational instrument) and new types of ships such as the **caravel**. It also spurred Europeans to open up new maritime routes, including to the Americas.

WHERE DOES PEPPER COME FROM?

Harvesting pepper is a delicate job. Black pepper is a climbing vine that thrives in tropical climates. The flower spikes that grow on the vine produce small, round berries. After they're picked, the spikes are laid out in the sun for several days to dry. The dried peppercorns are then ready to use.

Other species belonging to the pepper plant family produce different types of pepper:

- **Cubeb** (or tailed pepper), which produces green berries that are harvested and dried, and has a stronger taste than black pepper
- **Long pepper,** cultivated for its male flower spikes, which are harvested and dried

- **Wild pepper**, which grows mainly on the island of Madagascar and only in the wild

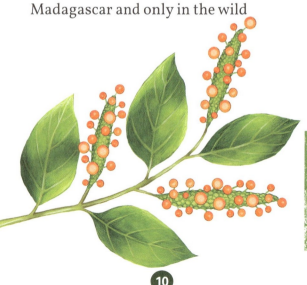

In the special-effects section of Honeydukes candy shop, Harry Potter discovers Pepper Imps, which make you breathe fire.

WHAT ABOUT GRAY PEPPER?

Gray pepper is sold only in powder form. It's just ground black pepper. So why is it gray? When black peppercorns are ground up, the black skin mixes with the white berry. Mix black and white and you get gray. It's as simple as that!

While pepper isn't as valuable as it once was, it's still one of the most widely used spices in the world. It's a key ingredient in countless recipes, from appetizers to desserts. Some people even argue about its origins and whether a pepper is "true" or "false."

SOME MEMBERS OF THE TRUE PEPPER FAMILY ARE HIGHLY PRIZED. THEY INCLUDE:

- **Kampot pepper**, from Cambodia
- **Sarawak pepper**, from Malaysia
- **Malabar pepper**, from a coastal region of India known for producing the world's finest pepper
- **Bélem pepper**, from Brazil
- **Penja pepper**, from Cameroon

THERE ARE FALSE PEPPERS

Some spices taste like pepper but don't actually come from the pepper plant.

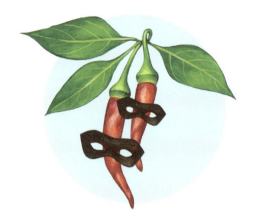

Pink pepper is the fruit (berry) of a South American tree called the false pepper. It belongs to the same family as the pistachio tree.

Cayenne pepper is a small hot pepper that's dried before being ground into a powder.

Guinea pepper is also known as melegueta pepper or grains of paradise.

Boreal pepper is less common but has been used for centuries by Indigenous people in Canada.

Dune pepper is the fruit of the green alder tree. It looks and tastes a lot like the berries of the pepper plant.

THE STUFF OF LEGENDS

Long ago it was thought that the lands where pepper plants grew were jealously guarded by snakes. The only way to harvest the berries was to scare away the snakes by setting fire to the plants. That's the reason peppercorns were said to be black.

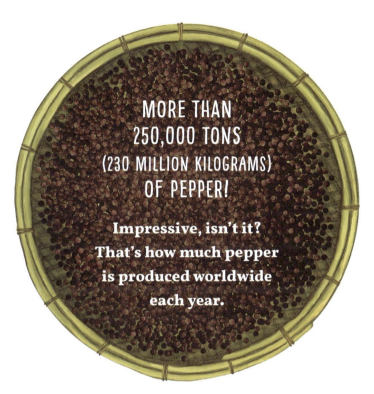

MORE THAN 250,000 TONS (230 MILLION KILOGRAMS) OF PEPPER!

Impressive, isn't it? That's how much pepper is produced worldwide each year.

A RISKY EXPERIMENT

If you hold a dish of ground pepper under your nose, it won't be long before the tingling, burning and sneezing set in. Blame it on the *piperine,* a compound in the pepper plant that causes a tingly nose in anyone who gets too close. For the pepper plant, it's a defense mechanism that helps keep harmful fungi away.

CHILI PEPPER

ITS ORIGIN

The chili pepper was a staple of the South American diet for thousands of years. Christopher Columbus is said to have brought it back to Europe on one of his voyages.

WHAT IS IT?

When you think about the chili pepper, you automatically think of a burning mouth and watery eyes.

But there's more to the chili pepper than that. Surprisingly, it belongs to the same family as the tomato, eggplant, potato and green pepper. The chili pepper is a *pod* that comes from the fruit of five different species of plants. It grows in a variety of colors (green, red, yellow, orange) and has seeds.

The chili pepper also comes in different sizes, shapes and flavors. The individual species can be identified by their flowers (purple, white, green or even spotted with red and yellow).

Paprika is the name given to the red bell pepper in Hungary. Dried and ground, it yields a spice of the same name. Sweet paprika is obtained by removing more than half the seeds. Hot paprika contains a larger proportion of seeds and stems. In Hungary paprika is used instead of pepper at the dinner table.

The *Aztecs* drank a beverage made from chili peppers mixed with cocoa.

WHY DOES IT BURN?

The culprit is *capsaicin*. This strange-sounding name refers to the substance found in the seeds of the chili pepper. The more capsaicin there is in the seeds, the hotter the pepper. Only reptiles and birds are immune to capsaicin, eating pepper seeds without a care in the world.

Capsaicin is so strong that it will burn not only your mouth but also your fingers if you're not careful. So take precautions when handling the hottest chili peppers!

SOME PEPPER VARIETIES

From the mildest to the hottest, there's a pepper for everyone.

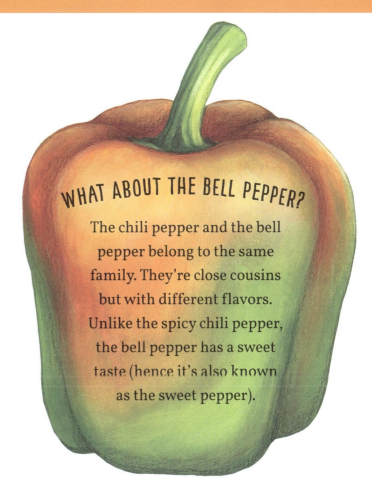

WHAT ABOUT THE BELL PEPPER?

The chili pepper and the bell pepper belong to the same family. They're close cousins but with different flavors. Unlike the spicy chili pepper, the bell pepper has a sweet taste (hence it's also known as the sweet pepper).

Mild peppers, such as paprika and ancho

Medium peppers, such as Espelette or cayenne

Hot peppers, such as the bird pepper (peri peri)

Superhot peppers, such as the habanero and the Naga, one of the hottest on the planet

MUSTARD

WHERE DOES IT COME FROM?

Before it ends up in jars and squeeze bottles, mustard starts off as a plant. It belongs to the same family as the cabbage, turnip and radish. Its bright yellow flowers produce small seeds that range in color from yellowish-white to black.

ITS HISTORY

Mustard as we know it today first appeared when some curious person decided to mix ground mustard seed with unfermented grape juice, resulting in the condiment found on tables around the world.

The mustard plant is highly invasive but not harmful. It actually plays an important role in agriculture. Pollinating insects are drawn to its flowers, which produce a lot of **pollen** and **nectar**.

Its strong roots loosen the soil and absorb nitrogen, which improves the growing conditions for crops such as wheat and barley.

People have been eating mustard greens for a very long time. In the southern United States, mustard greens are harvested and simmered for several hours with turnip greens, bacon, lemon and vinegar.

HOW IS IT MADE?

1. The seeds are harvested.

2. They are stored before removing impurities.

3. The seeds are flattened between two rollers.

4. The crushed seeds are placed in a vat with vinegar and mixed for several hours.

6. The mixture is strained until smooth, then left to rest for at least three days until its bitter taste disappears.

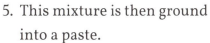

5. This mixture is then ground into a paste.

7. The resulting mustard can be flavored or kept plain.

There are many different recipes for mustard. But they're all made with one of three types of mustard seed.

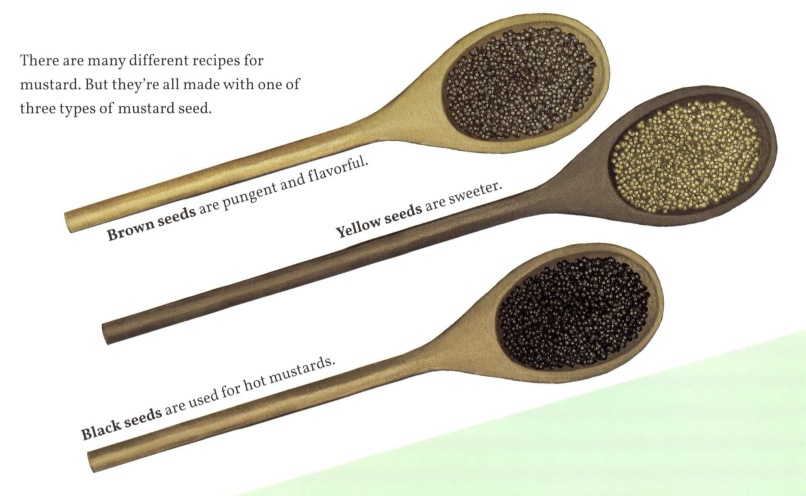

Brown seeds are pungent and flavorful.

Yellow seeds are sweeter.

Black seeds are used for hot mustards.

WHY DOES MUSTARD HAVE A PUNGENT FLAVOR THAT GOES UP YOUR NOSE?

Mustard seeds contain a natural substance that changes when it's ground and mixed with water.

This chemical reaction creates a new substance called ***allyl isothiocyanate***. When it comes into contact with the ***taste buds*** on the tongue, it sets off a chain reaction that causes a burning sensation in the throat and nose.

A MUSTARD FOR EVERY TASTE

From sweet to spicy to plain, there's a mustard for everyone!

ENGLISH MUSTARD

Superhot
Blend of yellow and brown mustard seeds

DIJON MUSTARD

Hot or extra hot
Blend of yellow and brown mustard seeds

OLD-FASHIONED MUSTARD

Four ingredients: whole brown mustard seeds, water, salt and vinegar

All sorts of ingredients can be added to mustard to create different varieties—honey, seaweed, tarragon, basil, walnuts and even violets or cinnamon and candied fruit (Italian mustard).

SWEET YELLOW MUSTARD

Sugar or caramel is sometimes added to give it a sweet taste.

The play *A Midsummer Night's Dream*, by 16th-century English playwright William Shakespeare, features a fairy character named Mustardseed.

GINGER

At first glance ginger isn't the most attractive of dinner guests, mostly because of its odd color and misshapen appearance. But it's finding its way into more and more kitchens.

WHAT IS IT?

Ginger is the **rhizome** (a type of **bud**) that grows on the roots of the ginger plant.

Ginger tastes different depending on where it comes from.

- **Jamaican ginger** has a delicate flavor. It's used raw in cooking and to flavor drinks.
- **African ginger** has a pungent flavor. It's prized for its essential oil.
- **Australian ginger** has a very sweet lemon flavor. It's used mainly in desserts.
- **Indian ginger** has a delicate lemon flavor. It's ground into a powder before it's used.

> Young rhizomes have a very mild flavor. But the bigger the rhizome, the spicier it tastes.

GINGER IN ALL ITS FORMS

Ginger comes in many different forms, depending on how it's used.

raw: eaten plain, peeled or unpeeled, grated or sliced

marinated in rice vinegar: used as a key ingredient in Japanese cuisine

candied: used in cookies and desserts such as gingerbread

powdered: used as a spice to enhance the flavor of certain dishes

SUGAR

Close your eyes and whisper the word *sugar* a few times. What comes to mind? Sweet thoughts or sour memories? Chances are, it's sweet thoughts. Unless, of course, too much sugar once turned your belly sour!

WHERE DOES IT COME FROM?

Sugar doesn't start off in granulated or cube form. It's first found in nature. Many plants are rich in natural sugars, including fruit, but also the maple tree, the **agave** plant and the date palm. And honey is actually made by bees, which turn the nectar from flowering plants into the sweet treat we know and love.

The sugar used in cooking comes mainly from two plants:
- **sugar beet**, grown in temperate climates
- **sugarcane**, grown in hot, humid climates

During **photosynthesis**, plants transform solar energy into a natural sugar called glucose. This nutrient concentrates in the roots of the sugar beet and the stalks of sugarcane.

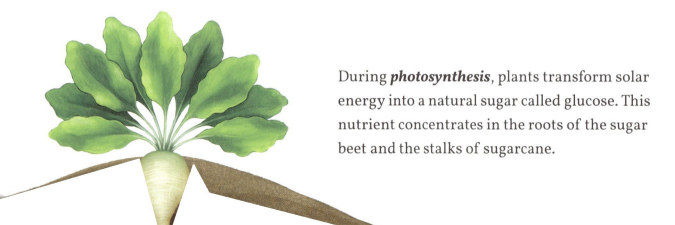

SUGAR IN ALL ITS FORMS

Sugar comes in many different forms. What's your favorite?

GRANULATED SUGAR

CASTER SUGAR

MOLASSES

ICING SUGAR
ROCK SUGAR

BROWN SUGAR

SYRUPS

- **Granulated sugar** is extracted from the sugar beet (white) or sugarcane (brown).
- **Caster sugar**, or berry sugar, is granulated sugar that's been sifted or ground into fine crystals.
- **Icing sugar** is granulated sugar that's been reduced to a very fine white powder.
- **Rock sugar** is a very pure form of sugar made from sugar syrup.
- **Brown sugar** is an amber-colored granulated sugar obtained from sugarcane juice.
- **Molasses** is the thick, dark syrup left over after sugar has been refined.
- **Syrups** such as maple (made from the boiled sap of the sugar maple tree), agave and corn are also very popular.

SUGARING OFF!

Sugaring off is an annual Canadian tradition that celebrates maple syrup and other maple products:
- maple sugar
- maple taffy
- maple butter

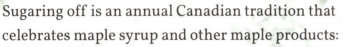

HOW IS SUGAR MADE?

The first step is to extract the juice from the plant.

The juice of the sugar beet comes from the root.

The beet root is cut into thin strips, then mixed with lukewarm water until a juice forms.

The juice of the sugarcane comes from the stalk.

The sugarcane stalk is cut into pieces and ground up.

Almost the same production method is used for both plants.

1. The juice is filtered to remove the impurities.

2. The juice is then boiled in a series of boilers until a syrup forms.

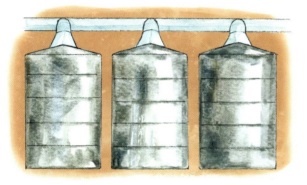

3. Fine crystals (icing sugar) are added to crystallize the syrup.

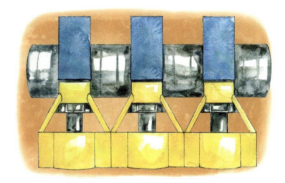

4. The syrup is strained in centrifuges.

5. Then it is poured into turbines with wire screen baskets. The turbines spin really fast, acting like giant lettuce spinners, to drain off the syrup and leave the crystallized sugar behind on the walls of the baskets.

6. The sugar is dried, then transformed into powder or lumps.

The sugar from sugar beets is naturally white. The sugar from sugarcane is naturally brown.

CINNAMON

Can anyone resist a warm cinnamon roll? Of course, if you're not a fan of cinnamon, you probably wouldn't have any trouble. As the saying goes, there's no accounting for taste. Regardless, cinnamon is a fascinating spice.

WHAT IS CINNAMON?

Cinnamon is the bark of the small cinnamon tree. It's typically found in Sri Lanka and Indonesia but also in Madagascar and Brazil.

There are two types of cinnamon trees:

- **Ceylon cinnamon** (Sri Lanka) has very thin, brittle bark that's orange-ochre in color. It's very sweet and fragrant.

- **Chinese cinnamon** (grown mainly in Indonesia) has thick bark that's orange-brown in color. It's not particularly sweet but rather a bit bitter.

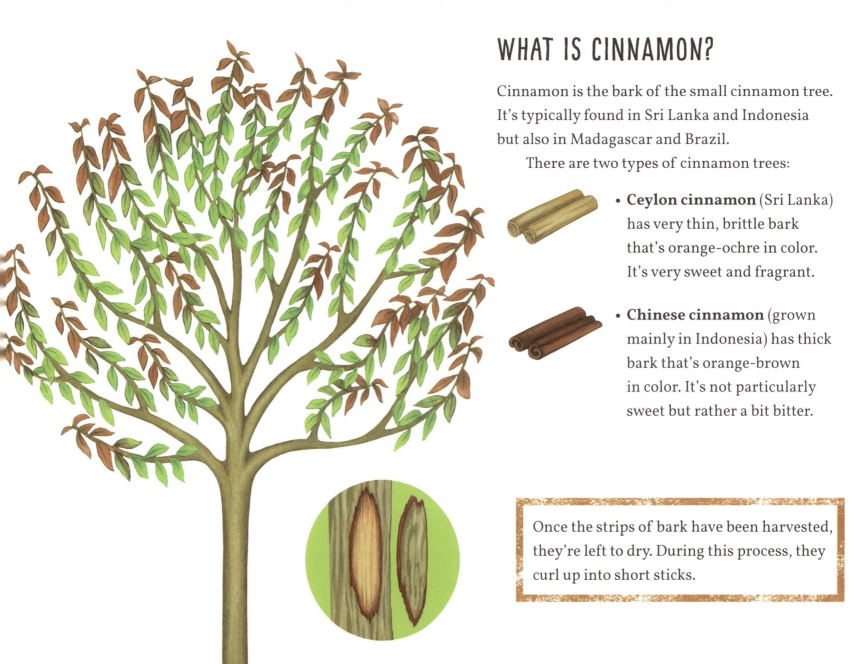

Once the strips of bark have been harvested, they're left to dry. During this process, they curl up into short sticks.

Cinnamon is a popular ingredient in many desserts because of its warm, sweet flavor. But cinnamon can also be used in savory dishes like spaghetti sauce, *tagine* and chili.

Cinnamon extract is used to flavor foods such as candy and chewing gum, and personal hygiene products like toothpaste. It's also used in perfumes.

Cinnamon is one of the oldest known spices. It was originally used in religious ceremonies and medicine. Later, as a precious commodity reserved for the rich, it was used to disguise the unpleasant smell of food that had gone bad.

VANILLA

WHERE DOES IT COME FROM?

Vanilla is the fruit of the vanilla plant, a tropical climbing vine from Central America that belongs to the orchid family.

Before a flower can produce fruit, it needs to be pollinated. The transfer of pollen from the **stamen** of one flower to the **pistil** of another flower is what results in fruit. The wind, bees, small birds like the hummingbird, butterflies (especially the monarch) and other insects are the key players in the **pollination** process.

For years, vanilla plants grown outside Central America did not bear fruit. They were considered ornamental plants until growers realized they didn't have the pollinating insects found in Central America. Without these pollinators, fertilization could not take place. That's when growers began using artificial pollination methods, depositing pollen grains by hand onto the pistil, the female part of the vanilla plant.

THE FRUIT OF THE VANILLA TREE

A vanilla bean is actually a green pod measuring 4.5 to 6 inches (12 to 15 centimeters) long and containing thousands of tiny seeds.

In 1841 Edmond Albius, a young slave from Réunion Island, used his powers of observation to figure out how to artificially fertilize the flowers of the vanilla plant by pollinating the flower's pistil by hand. He invented the technique by watching pollinating insects at work.

FROM POD TO TABLE

1. The green vanilla pods are harvested when the tips start to turn yellow.

   As they dry, they turn dark brown or black in color. Several steps are needed to bring out the full aroma and flavor.

2. **Blanching**: The pods are dipped in hot water for a few minutes.

3. **Sweating**: The pods are spread out between layers of woolen blankets; they are then placed in large, open crates for about 10 hours to dry and blacken.

4. **Drying**: The pods are left to dry in the sun for two to six weeks.

5. **Curing**: The pods are sealed in wooden chests and left to ferment for several months to develop their flavor.

VANILLA COMES IN DIFFERENT FORMS

There are different types of vanilla, including Mexican vanilla, Madagascar vanilla (bourbon vanilla) and Tahitian vanilla.
- **vanilla bean**: fresh and whole, stored in a glass tube
- **vanilla powder**: dried vanilla beans ground into a fine powder
- **vanilla sugar**: a blend of sugar and dried vanilla extract
- **vanilla extract**: the solution obtained from soaking vanilla beans in alcohol

CHOCOLATE

Chocolate comes from the cacao tree, a shrub native to Central America. Its oval-shaped fruit, the cocoa pod, can be yellow or orange and is filled with sticky blue seeds, or beans. Without cocoa pods, there would be no chocolate!

There are several types of cocoa pods, but the most highly prized are:
- forastero
- Trinitario
- criollo

Each type produces a distinctive flavor of cocoa.

The cacao tree has been cultivated for centuries. The **Maya** and the Aztecs used cocoa beans to make a chocolate drink. They used cocoa butter as a balm to treat burns and chapped skin.

FROM POD TO SHELF

There are many steps involved in making chocolate.

1. **Harvesting**: The pods are harvested twice a year, in December and July.

2. **Breaking**: The pods are split open to collect the seeds.

3. **Drying**: The seeds are spread out on banana leaves and left in the sun for two weeks. The fermented seeds become cocoa beans.

4. **Winnowing and roasting**: The beans are sorted, agitated to remove their outer shells and roasted for about 30 minutes.

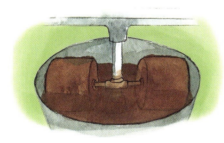

5. **Grinding**: The beans are ground into a rich, fatty paste (cocoa paste), from which cocoa butter is extracted.

6. **Blending**: The cocoa paste is mixed with sugar and cocoa butter. This mixture is then ground into a refined, melt-in-your-mouth paste known as chocolate.

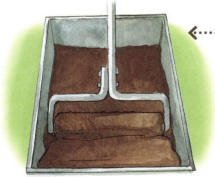

7. **Conching**: The chocolate is worked for a long time until it is smooth and creamy.

8. **Processing**: The chocolate is ready to be flavored and made into other products to be sold.

A CHOCOLATE FOR EVERY TASTE

Dark chocolate is a blend of cocoa, cocoa butter and sugar. Its flavor varies depending on the cocoa content:
- **Less than 65 percent cocoa** results in a sweet chocolate.
- **Between 65 and 70 percent cocoa** produces a slightly bitter chocolate.
- **80 percent cocoa** yields a harder chocolate with a pronounced bitter taste.
- **90 percent cocoa** or more results in a very bitter chocolate.

White chocolate is a blend of cocoa, milk (17 percent), sugar and cocoa butter (20 percent), processed to create a milder flavor. Vanilla is sometimes added. White chocolate does not contain **caffeine**. The amount of caffeine in chocolate depends on the type of bean used and the degree of fermentation.

Milk chocolate is a blend of cocoa, cocoa butter, powdered milk and sugar.

Milk chocolate was first created in Vevey, Switzerland, in 1875.

CHOCOLATE COMES IN MANY SHAPES

- dark, milk or white chocolate **bars**, to which ingredients like hazelnuts, puffed rice, dried fruit and coffee beans are sometimes added
- cocoa **powder**, which is mixed with water or milk to make hot chocolate
- **hazelnut spreads**
- chocolate **desserts**

Chocolate can be harmful to some animals, including cats, dogs, parrots and horses.

The tradition of making chocolate sculptures is very popular, especially during the holidays.

COFFEE

WHERE DOES IT COME FROM?

Coffee beans come from the fruit of a tropical shrub called the coffee plant. The fleshy, bright-red, purple or yellow fruit, known as the coffee cherry, has two seeds that lie flat against each other. Each seed contains one green coffee bean.

Coffee is one of the most popular beverages in the world. It's estimated that more than two billion cups of coffee are consumed every day.

THERE ARE TWO MAIN TYPES OF COFFEE BEANS:

- **Arabica beans** produce a mellow, aromatic coffee. They are fragile and grow best at higher altitudes.
- **Robusta beans** are slightly more bitter and contain twice as much caffeine. They are grown mainly in low-lying areas.

Some coffees are highly prized:
- **Bourbon pointu** from Réunion Island
- **Blue Mountain** from Jamaica

ITS ORIGINS

Coffee as a beverage is thought to have originated in Yemen between the 12th and 15th centuries. Venetian merchants introduced it to Europe around 1600, after which its popularity skyrocketed. In 1689 the first coffee shop was opened in Boston. In 1890 David Strang of New Zealand invented and patented soluble coffee powder. By 1938 the French company Nestlé refined the process and started selling Nescafé, the instant coffee still popular today.

According to an ancient legend, an Ethiopian goatherd noticed that his goats would stay awake all night after eating the fruit of a particular shrub. He shared his observation with some local monks, who are said to have chewed the berries as a way to stay awake during their prayers.

The world's top coffee-producing countries are Brazil, Vietnam, Colombia, Indonesia, Ethiopia and Honduras.

FROM BEAN TO CUP

There are many steps involved in producing coffee. First the fruit is picked once it reaches peak ripeness.

1. **Harvesting** is done by hand. Only the ripest coffee cherries are picked.

2. **Destemming** consists of removing all the cherries from each branch.

To extract the coffee beans, the cherries are stripped of their fleshy outer skin. This process is made up of several steps:

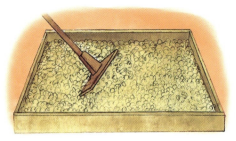 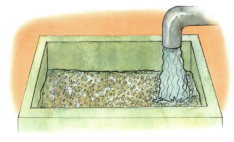

3. **Drying**: The coffee cherries are spread out and regularly raked over until their skin dries out and crumbles.

4. **Washing**: The skin is pierced and the ripe coffee cherries are soaked in water until the fleshy pulp breaks down to reveal the coffee beans inside.

5. **Sorting:** The rotten, damaged and discolored coffee beans are picked out. The beans are then hulled to remove their parchment-like skin and the husks are collected for fuel.

6. **Roasting:** During this final step, the coffee beans are roasted at high temperatures to develop their flavor. They double in size and change from green to brown or black.

The way that coffee is brewed has evolved over time. From the oldest method—ground coffee steeped in boiling water—to fancy coffee makers with prefilled pods and brew selectors, there are many ways to brew coffee.

drip coffee maker (manual or electric)

French press (plunger) coffee maker

Italian espresso maker (Moka Express)

espresso machine

CAFFEINATED OR DECAFFEINATED?

Coffee contains caffeine, a stimulant you shouldn't have too much of. A technology exists that can remove up to 99 percent of the caffeine from coffee beans.

THERE ARE TWO WAYS TO MAKE DECAFFEINATED COFFEE.

- a chemical method that uses solvents
- a natural method that uses water and activated charcoal

This step is done before roasting, when the coffee beans are still green.

FAIR TRADE COFFEE

Fair trade coffee is produced, harvested and sold in ways designed to meet several standards:

- guarantee farmers the best market price
- provide safe and respectful working conditions
- comply with environmental regulations

TEA

WHERE DOES IT COME FROM?

Tea has been grown in China and India for more than 4,000 years. It was brought to Europe in the 1500s. These days it's consumed all over the world.

Tea is a beverage made by steeping the dried leaves of the tea tree in water. The tea tree is a shrub native to East Asia. There are three main varieties of tea tree, depending on where they grow: China, Southeast Asia or India. The tea tree is kept pruned to a maximum height of three feet (one meter). This makes picking easier and improves the quality of the tea, since older leaves tend to produce less flavorful tea.

According to legend, tea was first discovered in 2737 BCE, when Chinese emperor Shennong requested a cup of hot water to quench his thirst. As the water was boiling, leaves from a nearby wild tree blew into the pot. The emperor is said to have found the new beverage delightful.

FROM PLANTATION TO CUP

The quality of tea depends on how it's harvested. The best teas come from the plucking method—picking the bud and the first two or three tender green leaves. The darker leaves farther down the stem produce progressively less complex teas. Before they can be used, tea leaves must be processed. Depending on the method used, this results in black, green, oolong or white tea. The most straightforward teas require only one or two steps.

Black tea is the most popular in North America. Its production is a five-step process:

1. **Withering** allows the excess moisture to evaporate from the tea leaves.

2. **Rolling** destroys the inner membranes of the leaves and releases their compounds.

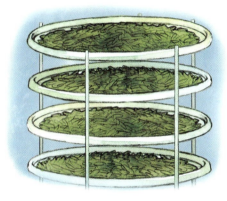

3. **Fermentation** takes place in a moist environment to develop the tea's flavor and coppery color.

4. **Drying** halts the fermentation process and eliminates moisture. The tea leaves are exposed to a temperature of 194°F (90°C).

5. **Sorting** separates the tea leaves according to quality.

Green tea is unfermented. The leaves are steamed for a few minutes at a high temperature, then rolled and dried. It's the most popular type of tea in Asia.

Oolong tea, halfway between black and green tea, is semi-fermented. The leaves are simultaneously stirred and fermented at a high temperature.

White tea, which is very rare, undergoes almost no processing after being picked. It is harvested in spring, and only the buds and the first two or three leaves are used. They're dried in the shade for a few days.

The subtle, delicate aroma of **jasmine tea** is obtained by covering tea leaves overnight with closed jasmine buds. As dusk falls, the petals open up, infusing the tea leaves beneath with their fragrance.

Herbal teas are tea leaves infused with spices, orange peel, bergamot or flowers. Dried tea leaves are sprayed with natural essential oils of flowers or fruits.

THE TEA EXPERIENCE

Nowadays people the world over drink tea without a second thought. But in some countries, tea drinking is steeped in tradition. The British are famous for their **afternoon tea**, and the question of when to add the milk to the cup—before or after the tea—is a hot topic among British tea enthusiasts.

In Chinese and Japanese cultures, serving and drinking tea is an art form. In Japan the **tea ceremony** is a sacred ritual that unfolds in a series of very precise steps, using special objects.

GLOSSARY

agave—a plant native to the hot, dry regions of the Americas and the Caribbean. The nectar of some species is used as a sweetener.

allyl isothiocyanate—a chemical compound present in mustard that gives it its pungency

astrolabe—an ancient astronomical instrument used by sailors to navigate by calculating the height of the stars above the horizon

Aztecs—a Nahuatl-speaking people who founded the Mexican empire in the 15th century

bud—the small growth from which leaves and flowers appear

caffeine—a stimulant that occurs naturally in coffee, tea and cocoa (in small amounts)

capsaicin—a chemical compound found in chili peppers that produces a burning sensation in the mouth

caravel—a small, light sailing vessel invented by the Portuguese in the 15th century for long maritime voyages

chili—a pungent hot pepper often ground into a dark-red, powdered spice blend widely used in South American cuisine

fair trade—a way of buying and selling products that is designed to ensure that small producers receive a fair price for their goods

gastronomy—the field of knowledge related to food and cooking

Maya—an ancient people from Mexico and Central America whose culture is still present in Mexico today. Descendants of the Maya live in Guatemala, Belize and the Mexican state of Yucatán.

nectar—the sugary liquid in flowers that attracts bees, which collect it

photosynthesis—the process by which plants transform solar energy into nutrients by absorbing carbon dioxide from the air and releasing oxygen

piperine—the compound that gives pepper its spicy, pungent flavor

pistil—the female part in the center of a flower that forms fruit and produces seeds

pod—the protective outer skin that contains the seeds

pollen—the fine powder produced by the male part of a flower that causes the female part of the same type of flower to produce seeds

pollination—the phenomenon in which pollen is transferred from the male part of the flower to the female part of the flower

rhizome—a type of plant stem that grows underground horizontally and can produce the shoot and root system of a new plant

salting—the use of dry edible salt to preserve certain foods

salt marshes—areas of low, flat, poorly drained ground that are regularly flooded by salt water due to tidal movement

stamen—the male part of the flower, which produces pollen

tagine—a slow-cooked North African meat stew named after the clay pot in which it's cooked

taste buds—tiny bumps on the tongue that detect the five main tastes: sweet, salty, sour, bitter and savory (umami)

tides—the rise and fall of ocean levels caused by the gravitational pull of the moon and sun, and Earth's rotation

INDEX

agave plant, 22, 23, 42
agriculture: pollinators, 16, 28, 43; and tea plantations, 38
allyl isothiocyanate, 18, 42
Australia, 3, 20
Aztecs, 14, 30, 42

beets, sugar, 22–25
bell peppers, 14, 15
beverages: of Aztecs, 14, 30; coffee, 34–37; hot chocolate, 33; tea, 38–41
black pepper: history and types of, 8–11; and piperine, 13, 42; similar tasting plants, 12; use of, 13
boreal pepper, 12
British afternoon tea, 41
buds, 20, 40, 42

caffeine, 32, 37, 42
Canada, 12, 24
capsaicin, 15, 42
cayenne pepper, 12, 15
chili peppers: about, 3, 14–15, 42; and capsaicin, 15, 42; cayenne pepper, 12, 15
China: history, 2, 8, 38; tea ceremony, 41
chocolate, 30–33
cinnamon, 8, 26–27
cocoa butter, 30, 31, 32
coffee: history and types of, 34–35; making, 37; processing, 36
corn syrup, 23
cultures: hospitality, 2, 41; legends, 2, 13, 35, 38

date palm, 22
desserts, 21, 27, 33
dune pepper, 12

environment: deforestation, 38; deicing alternatives, 7; fair trade products, 37, 42
Ethiopia, 35
European trade, 8, 9, 14, 35, 38
extracts, 27, 29

fair trade products, 37, 42
fleur de sel, 3, 4
food preservation, salting, 7, 43
France, 2, 3

gastronomy, 4, 42
ginger, 8, 20–21
green alder trees, 12
Guinea pepper, 12

Hawaiian salt, 3
health: and caffeine, 37; cocoa risk to pets, 33; and salt, 6, 7
Himalayan pink salt, 5
honey, 22
hot mustard, 18, 19
hot peppers, 3, 12, 14–15
Hungary, 14

India, 8, 38

Japan, tea ceremony, 41

maple syrup, 22, 23, 24
Maya, 30, 42
molasses, 23
mustard: and allyl isothiocyanate, 18, 42; history and types of, 16, 18, 19; processing, 17
mustard greens, 16

Nescafé instant coffee, 35

paprika, 14
pepper (peppercorns): history and types of, 8–11; and piperine, 13, 42; similar-tasting plants, 12; use of, 13
photosynthesis, 22, 42
pink pepper (false pepper), 12
piperine, 13, 42
pods: about, 42; types, 14, 28, 30
pollination, 16, 28, 43

rhizomes, 20, 43
rock salt, 3, 5
Roman soldiers, 2
Russia, 2

salt: history and types of, 2–3; production, 4–5; uses, 5, 6–7
salting of food, 6, 43
salt marshes, 3, 4, 43
saltwater lakes, 5
savory dishes, 27
sea salt, 3, 4, 5
sense of smell, 1, 13
shipping, trade, 8, 9, 14, 35, 38
spices: burning sensation, 15, 18; as currency, 2, 8; history of, 8–9
sugar beets, 22–25
sugarcane, 22–25
sweet peppers (bell), 14, 15
Switzerland, 32

tagine, 27, 43
taste buds, 1, 15, 18, 43
tea: history and types of, 38, 40; processing, 39; traditions, 41
trade routes, 8, 9, 14, 35, 38

vanilla, 28–29

Text copyright © Jacques Pasquet 2024
Illustrations copyright © Claire Anghinolfi 2024
Translation copyright © Ann Marie Boulanger 2024

Published in Canada and the United States in 2024 by Orca Book Publishers.
Originally published in French in 2020 by Isatis under the
title *Sucré, Salé, Poivré et Compagnie*.
orcabook.com

All rights are reserved, including those for text and data mining, AI training and similar technologies. No part of this publication may be reproduced or transmitted in any form or by any means, electronic or mechanical, including photocopying, recording or by any information storage and retrieval system now known or to be invented, without permission in writing from the publisher. The publisher expressly prohibits the use of this work in connection with the development of any software program, including, without limitation, training a machine learning or generative artificial intelligence (AI) system.

Library and Archives Canada Cataloguing in Publication

Title: Salt, pepper, season, spice : all the flavors of the world / Jacques Pasquet ; illustrated by Claire Anghinolfi ; translated by Ann Marie Boulanger.
Other titles: Sucré, salé, poivré et compagnie. English
Names: Pasquet, Jacques, 1948– author. | Anghinolfi, Claire, illustrator. | Boulanger, Ann Marie, translator.
Description: Translation of: Sucré, salé, poivré et compagnie. | Includes index.
Identifiers: Canadiana (print) 20230572839 | Canadiana (ebook) 20230572847 | ISBN 9781459839984 (hardcover) | ISBN 9781459839991 (PDF) | ISBN 9781459840003 (EPUB)
Subjects: LCSH: Flavor—Juvenile literature. | LCSH: Spices—Juvenile literature. | LCSH: Food—Juvenile literature. | LCGFT: Informational works.
Classification: LCC TX406 .P37 2024 | DDC j641.3/383—dc23

Library of Congress Control Number: 2023949579

Summary: This illustrated nonfiction book for middle-grade readers explores the spices, condiments and confections we love and the rich histories and cultures they come from around the world.

Orca Book Publishers is committed to reducing the consumption of nonrenewable resources in the production of our books. We make every effort to use materials that support a sustainable future.

Orca Book Publishers gratefully acknowledges the support for its publishing programs provided by the following agencies: the Government of Canada, the Canada Council for the Arts and the Province of British Columbia through the BC Arts Council and the Book Publishing Tax Credit.

We acknowledge the financial support of the Government of Canada through the National Translation Program for Book Publishing, an initiative of the *Roadmap for Canada's Official Languages 2013-2018: Education, Immigration, Communities*, for our translation activities.

The authors and publisher have made every effort to ensure that the information in this book was correct at the time of publication. The authors and publisher do not assume any liability for any loss, damage, or disruption caused by errors or omissions. Every effort has been made to trace copyright holders and to obtain their permission for the use of copyrighted material. The publisher apologizes for any errors or omissions and would be grateful if notified of any corrections that should be incorporated in future reprints or editions of this book.

Cover and interior artwork by Claire Anghinolfi
Edited in-house by Kirstie Hudson
Translated by Ann Marie Boulanger

Printed and bound in South Korea.